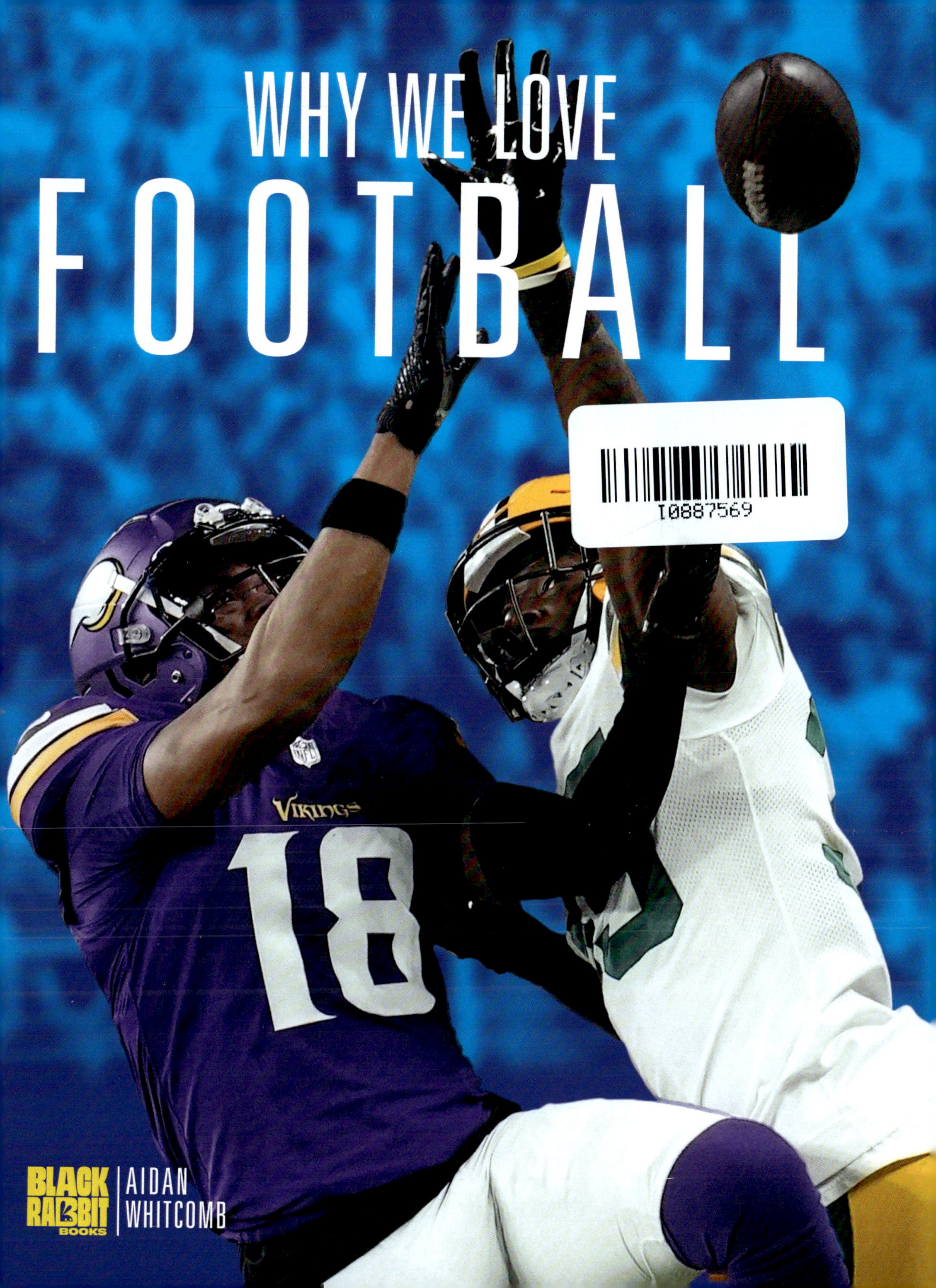

WHY WE LOVE FOOTBALL

AIDAN WHITCOMB

BLACK RABBIT BOOKS

TABLE OF CONTENTS

1

Football's Founders

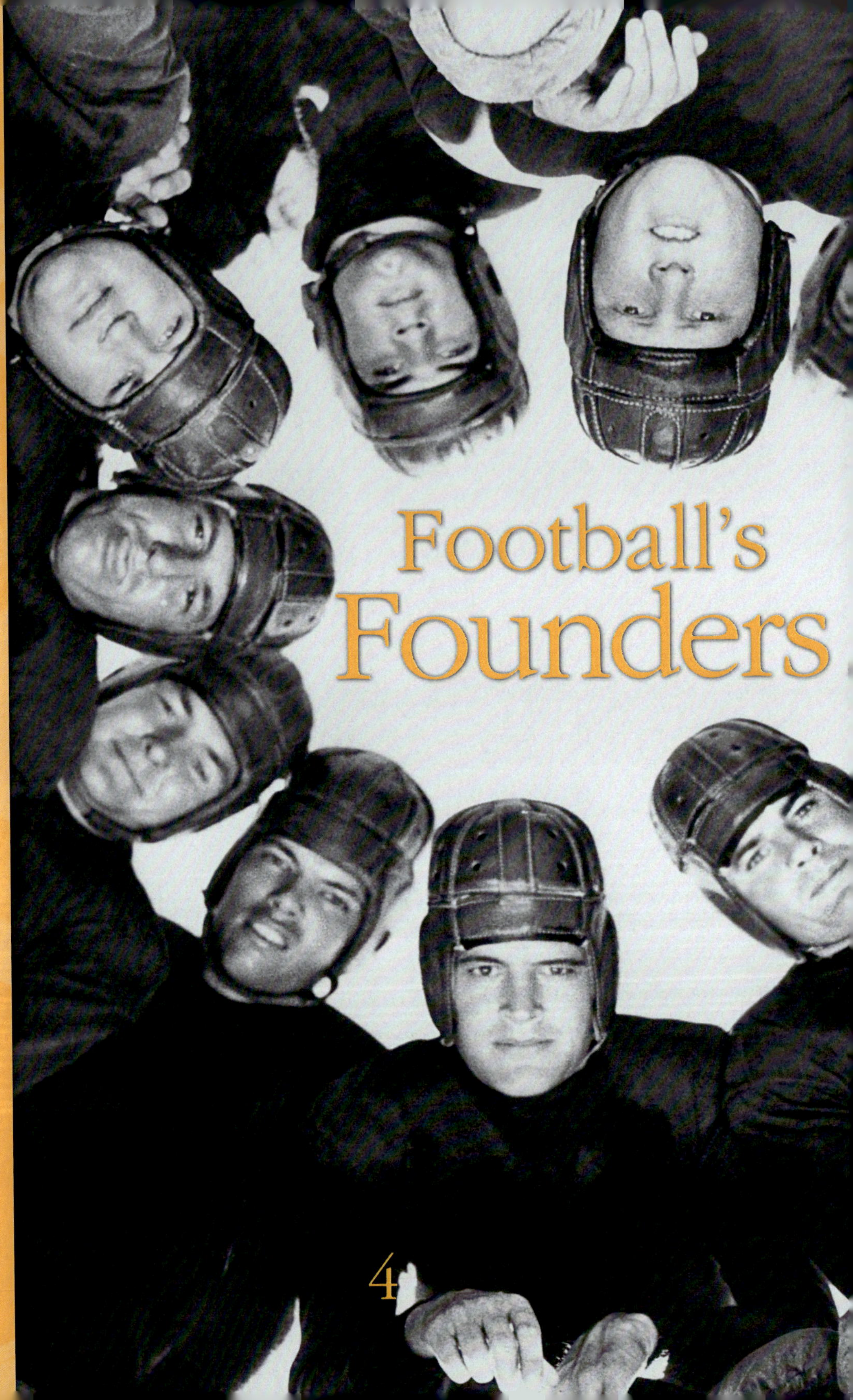

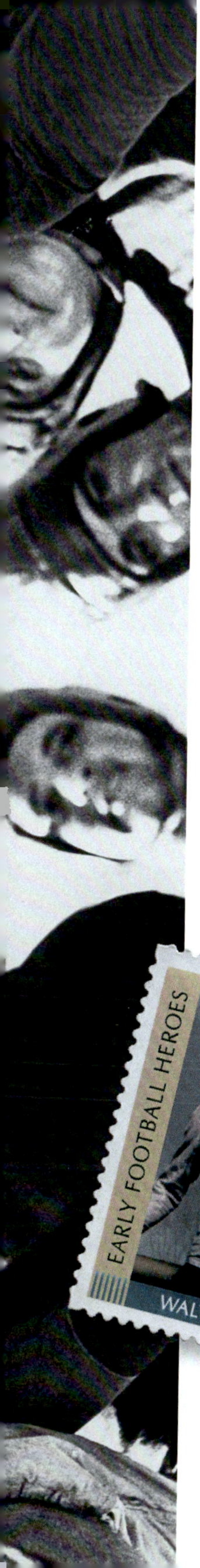

Football is an old sport. The first game was in 1869. Two college teams played. The game was similar to rugby and soccer. In 1880, Walter Camp updated the rules. He made football unique. The changes he made created the sport we know today.

In 1920, the National Football League (NFL) was created. Only 10 teams existed. Since then, the NFL has added more teams. There are now 32 teams. Millions of fans love the NFL. They love the sport's traditions.

Did You Know?

There are over 410 million NFL fans. It is the most watched sport in the United States.

2 Gameday at the Gridiron

Football is great to watch live. Games are full of energy. There is a lot of action. Fumbles and interceptions can change the game in a second. Long touchdowns get the crowd pumped up. The stadiums are lively. Fans cheer loudly. They celebrate every score.

Tailgating is a fun experience. It is a big party with other fans. It happens before the game. Fans gather in the parking lot. Many fans wear jerseys. There is great food. People play music. They get excited for the game.

Did You Know?

Arrowhead Stadium is home to the Kansas City Chiefs. It holds the record for the loudest stadium.

3

Football Favorites

Patrick Mahomes

NFL fans have many favorite players. There are superstars everywhere. Quarterbacks are often popular. Patrick Mahomes and Josh Allen are two greats. Fans love their skills. Sometimes they throw deep. Sometimes they run the ball. They can make great plays happen!

Fans also love wide receivers. Justin Jefferson is one of the best. His skills are incredible! He dives for catches. He makes one hand grabs. He scores many touchdowns. Fans love his celebrations, too.

Think About It What skills make a player great?

BILLS
ALLEN
17

4

Hard Hitters

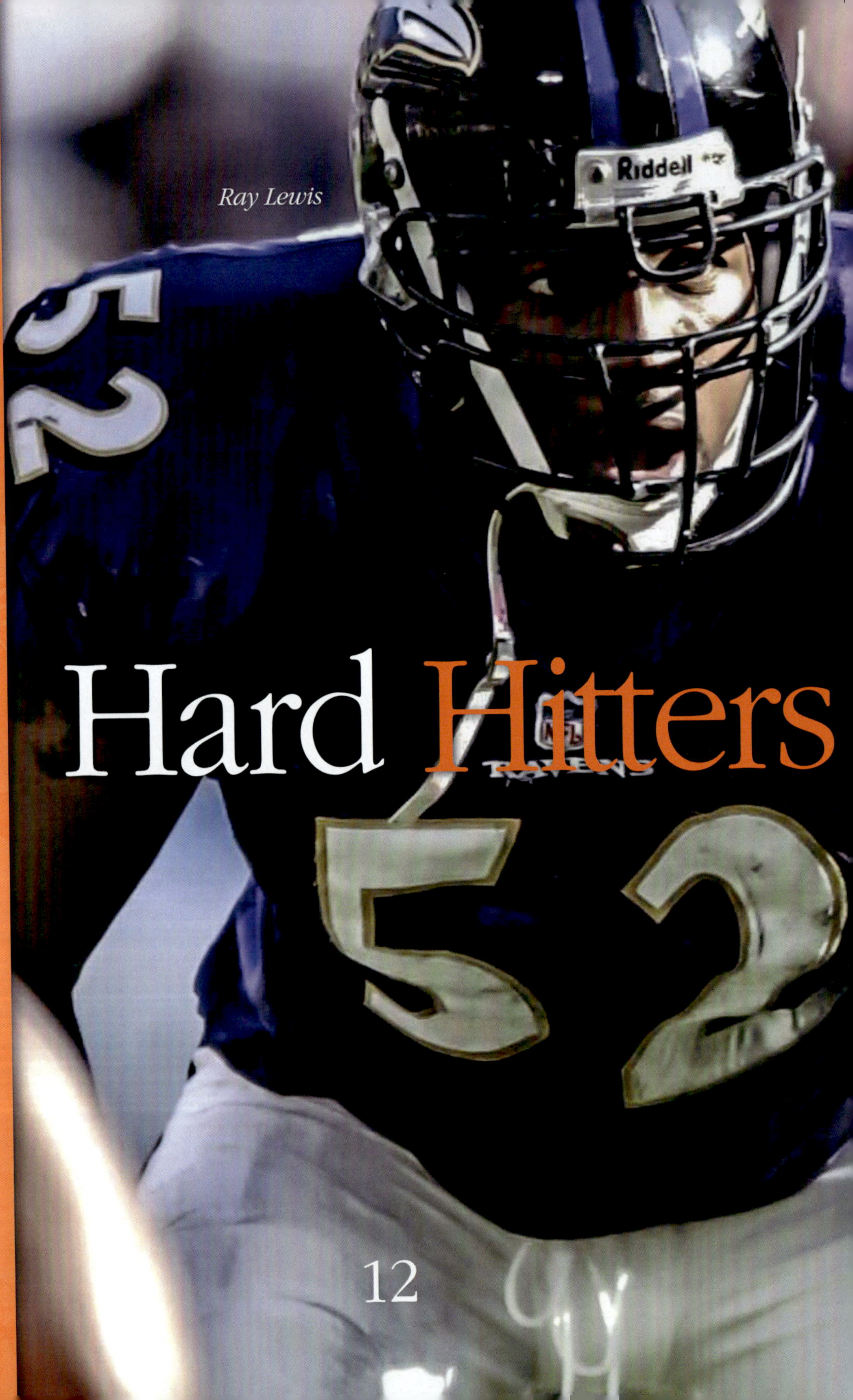

Ray Lewis

Fans love hard tackles. Defenders are so strong! Great tackles get the team excited. Some of the hardest hitters are linebackers. They stop everyone. They are also smart players. They lead the defensive line.

One legendary linebacker was Ray Lewis. He played for the Baltimore Ravens. He has the most career tackles. Lewis was athletic. He was also aggressive. He was hard to play against. Opponents feared him. He won many awards. Lewis is in the Hall of Fame.

Super Bowl Sunday

The Super Bowl is the NFL championship game. It is played in February. The best team from each conference competes. It is the biggest game of the year! The winning team gets championship rings.

Many fans watch the Super Bowl. Over 100 million people tune in! Some fans host parties. They cheer on the teams. Others enjoy the halftime show. Many famous musicians have performed. Rihanna and The Weeknd had memorable shows.

Did You Know?

The first Super Bowl was in 1967. The Green Bay Packers won it.

Rihanna

Super Bowl parties usually have lots of food to snack on while watching the game.

6

College Football Frenzy

College football is also very popular. The young players give each game their all. Today, more than 800 colleges have a football team. Students and alumni fill the stands. Many fans are very proud of their school. Many college stars go on to play in the NFL.

In 2014, the College Football Playoffs were created. Twelve teams play in the playoffs. Teams compete in bowl games, such as the Rose Bowl. The games are played around New Year's Day. Millions watch on TV.

14

MORE TO EXPLORE

FANTASTIC FACTS

The tallest NFL player ever was Richard Sligh at 7 feet (2.1 meters) tall.

Adrian Peterson once had 296 rushing yards, the most in a single game.

The Houston Texans are the newest NFL team. They entered the league in 2002.

Justin Tucker kicked a 66-yard (60.4-meter) field goal in 2021. It was the longest ever!

Peyton Manning has the most NFL MVP awards with five.

Chicago's Soldier Field is the oldest NFL stadium. It opened in 1924.

MORE TO EXPLORE

COOL COMPARISONS

Which quarterbacks have the most passing yards in NFL history?

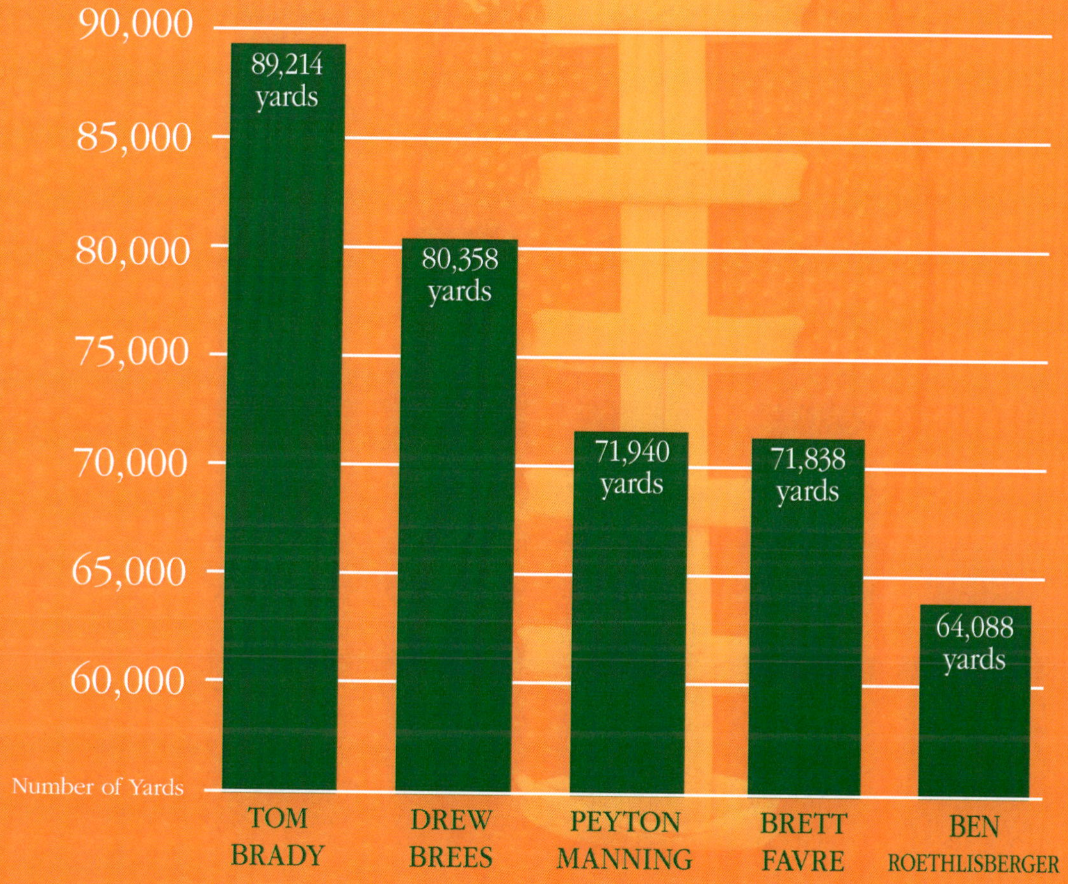

MORE TO EXPLORE

RESOURCES

Glossary

alumnus (uh-LUHM-nuhs) *plural*, alumni; Someone who was a student at a school.

conference (KON-fer-uhns) A group of sports teams from the same league that play against each other.

defensive line (dih-FEN-siv LAHYN) A group of three to four players who line up on the line of scrimmage and stop the player who has the ball.

interception (in-tur-SEP-shun) A catch made by a player from the opposing team.

opponent (uh-POH-nunt) A person, team, or group that is competing against another.

tradition (truh-DISH-uhn) A belief or custom handed down from one generation to another.

Read More

Blue, Tyler. *Stars of the NFL*. New York; London: Abbeville Kids, 2023.

Morey, Allan. *Patrick Mahomes*. Mankato, MN: Amicus Learning, 2025.

Silverman, Drew. *NFL Fan Favorites*. Mankato, MN: Black Rabbit Books, 2025.

Index

TOP RANK is published by Black Rabbit Books, P.O. Box 227, Mankato, MN, 56002. •

Top Rank is an imprint of Black Rabbit Books. • Designed by Danny Nanos • Photographs © Alamy Stock Photo/Cal Sport Media, 19; Associated Press/Abbie Parr cover, 1; Dreamstime/Aspenphoto, 6, Gerald T. Coli, 12–13; Getty Images/Andy Lewis/Icon Sportswire, 17, Bryan M. Bennett, 11, Chip Somodevilla, 15, David Berding, 10, Jamie Squire, 8–9, Jason O. Watson, 16, John Cordes/Icon Sportswire, 21, Perry Knotts, 2; Shutterstock/Everett Collection, 4–5, FeLopes, 7, Matushchak Anton, cover, 1, Ringo Chiu, 14, 20, Sean Locke Photography, 7, spatuletail, 5, Tatjana Baibakova, 18, WilleeCole Photography, 23

Library of Congress Cataloging-in-Publication Data: Names: Whitcomb, Aidan, author. | Title: Why we love football / Aidan Whitcomb. | Description: Mankato, MN : Top Rank, an imprint of Black Rabbit Books, 2026. | Series: Why we love sports | Includes bibliographical references and index. | Audience: Ages 8–11 | Audience: Grades 2–3 | Identifiers: LCCN 2024050030 | ISBN 9781644668047 (library binding) | ISBN 9781644668368 (paperback) | ISBN 9781644668689 (ebook) | Subjects: LCSH: Football—United States—Juvenile literature. | National Football League—Juvenile literature. | Football players—United States—Juvenile literature. | Classification: LCC GV950.7 .W495 2026 | DDC 796.332/64—dc23/eng/20241208 | LC record available at https://lccn.loc.gov/2024050030